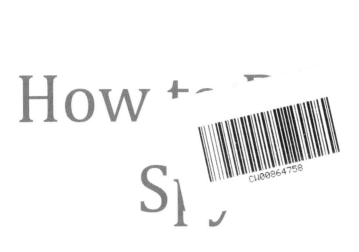

How to Spy

Tactical Espionage Acts, Intelligence and Counterintelligence Operational Techniques

Allain Verdugo

ISBN-13:
978-1974561834

ISBN-10:
1974561836

Operative vs Spy

Though in most cases the terms are interchangeable? That is not always so. An operative can just be a staff member in an organization conducting a clandestine or covert operation, which may or may not be related to spying. It just means, someone doing field work.

A spy or an asset is recruited by an intelligence officer (an officer can also be considered a spy) not only to steal secrets from the enemy camp but to engage in surreptitious deeds capable of causing havoc to the enemy. A spy may also engage in activities that can sabotage or mislead the enemy or even destroy the reputation of leaders by spreading false rumors or dis-information in places where they matter most and can do the most damage. The spy employs different ways to steal secrets. Some of the ways are:

Monitoring or surveillance: This involves using sophisticated intelligence equipment to observe the enemy from a safe distance. Before now, spies might have to disguise themselves to go into enemy territory or listen behind closed doors, but with the advancement of technology, modern covert surveillance methods now include using satellite photography, planting microphones, intercepting telephone calls, surreptitiously reading mail, and many other techniques. What used to be toys only meant for James Bond can now be bought in eBay. Don't get caught up with the tools though. Good old fashioned tradecraft will always be more important than fancy gadgets! The tools are there only to assist get what you want.

Larceny: This is relatively common among authors of detective novels. It involves a lot of risks which is the enemy in operations! It involves breaking and entering private property to steal secrets and other illegal acts. Risks are a given. But the idea is to find the least risky course of action, though it's the least sexy and least spy like. You want to cause an effect or steal information, not come up with an action packed movie sequence ala Mission Impossible!

The Insider: Intelligence officers use the word HUMINT when talking about intelligence collecting activities involving good old tradecraft. This is what a spy truly is at the core, or where the essence of spying came from. The word HUMINT stands for human intelligence (that is, intelligence collected by a human asset and not through high-tech electronic or technological means). This human intelligence asset (spy) can be planted as a confidant to infiltrate a group (a drug gang as used by the DEA or The FBI trying to break into a terrorist group). An inside spy could also be a member of an opposite group for instance the KGB passing information to the CIA. For instance, Aldrich (Rick) Ames, the CIA officer who made millions passing secrets to the Soviets while he drew his U.S. government paycheck. Or any other intelligence asset implanted, or recruited informants as a source of enemy intelligence. The insider spy will gain access to information in the form of rumors, documents and plans and divulge information to the agency he's working for.

Although the spy can be used for covert activities beyond stealing information, the intelligence agency must strike a balance between using spies for stealing secrets and information and the use of spies for covert actions. However, we will also tackle methods of recruitment of spies for activities that range from stealing secrets, spreading rumors and lies, bringing down the enemy through tricks and other destructive activities. Recruiting techniques of informants are kept hidden from the public by government intelligence agencies because they don't want the general population knowing how they recruit and use spies. This secrecy serves two purposes. Firstly, it makes it easy for government agencies to recruit ordinary citizens as spies because such people do not spot the warning signals that they are being recruited. Secondly, the secrecy helps a government ensure that its citizens don't start spying on it and finding out just how incompetent, and sometimes criminal, it (the government) can be. At its core, it's about manipulation of people and converting as many valuable assets to your cause. Be at peace with the M word (manipulation), because at the core, that is what the work is. Whether it is through intimidation, motivation, blackmail, seduction et cetera there are almost no rules in this game. Not everyone should be recruited or should know the agency or organization behind it. The CIA for example, uses different sorts of human assets and only a percentage of them know who they are working for. They may create layers upon layers of pretext and false entities to hide themselves. They are called deniable assets. As opposed to hidden assets, who operate in the shadows, but are directly tied to the CIA for example. Deniable assets are disavowed in case the operation gets sour. These assets can be in the know or were conned to serving a purpose, without them knowing who they're actually working for.

HOW TO FIND A SPY?

There are varying degrees of spy activities and each of this activity needs different types of individuals with different access, ability, personality and intelligence to effectively do the task at hand. The recruiter of these spies must know that each of these individuals become spies because of different motivating factors ranging from greed to need. Do also realize that the more you recruit, the more mistakes you can make in hiring the wrong person. Some are plants, implanted in place for the purpose of being recruited and a serving as a double agent.

The Unassuming Spy

This category of spies are most times unaware that they are giving out secrets, they do not set out to be spies and might give vital information away because they have a terrible sense of judgement, are lonely and need friends, have laid-back attitudes toward security. These individuals might be church members who always want to talk about business in church, or in bars with their colleagues. Intelligence officers like this source of information most because the risks are minimal to the intelligence officer, because the source does not know that they are passing sensitive information. Also be aware that the other party could be using this for disinformation. It is easy to implement for the enemy because of the minimal risk also.

The Traitor

The defector is one who leaves his post for another. It usually means abandoning your nationality for another. During the cold war, defectors provided most of the human intelligence resources. People defected because they are unsatisfied with the government and need a new place to stay or were eager for a new life. A defector provides information that they already have, and at the time of delivery, said information might not be useful anymore. Some defectors choose to stay and become a spy in place.

The Walk-In Spy

This type of spy is an individual that decides to work for a foreign power. For instance, John Walker, a U.S. Navy petty officer working as a code clerk, walked into the Soviet Embassy in Washington, D.C., carrying with him a collection of stolen documents as evidence of what he could provide. Walker was motivated purely by a desire to make money, and he eventually proved to be one of the most valuable spies the KGB ever ran. Walk-ins are basically traitors as they would sell out their own countries or organizations. Despite how valuable walk- in have proven to be, they are not to be trusted as they could be planted by the enemy to spread dis-information or steal information while feeding them confusing information at the same time. Walk-ins when caught face serious dangers or face treason charges. Like Penkovsky who was caught passing information to the British M16 for a year, was tried, found guilty and executed. Walk-ins don't just happen at the international political level. Anyone with a grudge against a commercial company, government agency, or political organization where he works can decide to take revenge by talking to someone willing to pay good money for good information.

The Bug

The bug is a spy deliberately placed in a position where he can gain employment in the camp of the enemy. This is also called undercover or placed assets. This operation involves a lot of risks for the operative ,and is also time consuming. But a well-placed asset is worth its weight in gold, with future intelligence items he can provide. It does require time and strong backstopping and legend creation to withstand background checks from the enemy organization. Even with false identification, it will take a long time for the Spy to gain the necessary promotions needed to get him to the desired position. This might take years, and the agent will be living a full or partial lie. The CIA has been known to develop up and coming talents or agents they expect will rise up in the ranks of the targeted government or organization. They hedge their bets and may take decades sometimes for their assets to be in place. They of course would help their candidates or assets rise up in the ranks. There is also the risk of the agent turning into a double agent. For example, a CIA asset is tasked to infiltrate ISIS. But that asset gets compromised and later decide to work for ISIS? A walk-in spy is actually easier to deal with than a planted spy in this regard.

The Enlistee

In some situations, the intelligence officer might have to recruit a spy if he is unable to get an inadvertent spy (an individual with loose lips who gives out information without being aware) or the risk of planting a spy is high and there are no defectors coming in. The recruit might not agree initially to spy for money. The case officer then has to seek other means of persuading the individual by looking for a weakness to exploit. This is really about human exploitation, and manipulation. There are virtually no restrictions and action or compliance is the only thing that matters; to make an asset provide intelligence or do your bidding.

The Doubled agent

Double agents are generally used to pass fake intelligence to the enemy, doubled spies can also provide information on the enemy's intelligence methods. When a defecting spy is caught, he will have to explain how he was recruited, how drops were made, how they were handled, who their handlers were, and all the other details of running spies (enemy agency's tradecraft). The spy who is caught, and then doubled, will also have to come clean about what damage he has already done. He will have to provide all the details on what kind of intelligence information he passed to the people he was spying for. This kind of information is so important, that even when a spy can't be doubled, it still pays to get him to talk. This is to know the level of damage the spy had done-- that's why intelligence agencies are always willing to plea bargain when they catch one of their own spying for the enemy.

Reasons Why People Become Spies

A case officer will have in his roster professional agents and other assets to work for him at the same time he looks for individuals with the potential, access, abilities he wants and tries to recruit them usually for a specific purpose or for an existing Op. When the op (eration) is done, the assets are let go. Often these individuals are not predisposed to this idea and this means that the case officer will have to use fraud and manipulation in order to recruit the regular people who have access to the wanted secrets. The case officer would have to make the potential recruit believe that his own personal interests will be best served if he becomes a traitor. That he would have to use emotional blackmail and every other trickery he possesses -- both good and bad tactics and strategies of persuasion and coercion.

A great way to make the recruit think that the case officer or the agent tasked to recruit assets is on his side, is for them to think they have the same ideals and goals. For instance, if the potential recruit lost a child before, through doctors' neglect and the hospital where the said recruit is working is being investigated? The case worker can convince the recruit that he is also going through the same ordeal thereby manipulating the recruit into thinking they have the same goals. Other ways include through promise of reward--which gives the recruit a reason to justify his treachery; prying on emotions such as anger, hatred, dissatisfaction, greed which could easily prompt the recruit into becoming a traitor.

Anger

This emotion is very powerful in recruiting a potential spy. The case officer still has a lot of work to do as anger might not be enough reason to motivate someone to become a traitor. An employee that has been passed for promotion, underpaid or feels he is not being treated fairly can turn into a traitor. Individuals who are angry at the system maybe because of injustice, religious differences, ideology or one who believes his leaders are incompetent and shouldn't be at the helms, might be good potential recruits.

Sex

When a potential recruit is in love or in an affair and the lover is in trouble? The potential recruit might be motivated through love. Honey pots, ravens and sparrows are intelligence operations using sex and love as tools of manipulation and intelligence extraction. The recruit (or intelligence target) who is already in love with the bait would fall for it and spill his guts or be manipulated to doing what the case officer wants.

Sex used in intelligence, according to Wikipedia:

"Love, honeypots, and recruitment

One previous CIA officer stated that while sexual entrapment wasn't normally an excellent tool to recruit a foreign official, it was in some cases utilized successfully to solve short-term issues. Seduction is a traditional technique; "swallow" was the KGB tradecraft term for ladies, and "raven" the term for guys, trained to seduce intelligence targets.

The Soviets utilized sex not only for direct recruitment, but as a contingency where an American officer may need to be compromised in the future. The CIA itself made minimal use of sexual recruitment versus foreign intelligence services. "Coercive recruitment generally didn't work. We discovered that offers of money and flexibility worked better".

The former KGB as you've seen are known for having agents specially trained in the art of seduction for the purposes of intelligence work. That is not to say other intelligence agencies and foreign powers do not employ these tactics and strategies. Although sex won't play a role in every recruitment, but it can make a critical difference in how successful many recruitments will be. Instead of having sex with the recruit, there are several different options for finding potential sex partners for the recruit to enjoy. This could include an ongoing affair (this may include blackmail), the use of prostitutes (who would have been given instructions on what to do), even the use of kinky sexual appetites, the use of a service agents specially trained to using sex to work the target. Sex and intelligence game is a dirty business and if the target has a special fetish? The rarer it is, the more it becomes a motivating factor. Sexual deviants into pedophilia and smut, will all be employed when necessary in the intelligence game. When lives are at stake? Unsanctioned, off the book child prostitutes will be exploited if absolutely necessary.

Fear

Another way of recruiting is through fear. This powerful force can be used to manipulate people into doing what they don't want to do. The potential recruit might be manipulated or blackmailed by the Case officers who have some dirt on them (the recruits). This can range from evidence of infidelity, fraud to inappropriate behavior such as molestation, sexual harassment or drug abuse. This dirt the case officer has on the recruit is the string he pulls to ensure he remains loyal. One treachery, leads to more. That first act of treachery alone will be enough to make that individual comply further on the threat that information will be revealed.

Using Force as Persuasion

When the life of loved ones or source of livelihood of the recruit is threatened, he might be forced to turn spy. People can be forced to spy. It's a technique that law enforcement agencies use all the time. They arrest a low-level drug dealer, prostitute, bookie, or some other petty criminal, then they threaten to put him in jail for many years unless he agrees to spy on more important criminals.

Trade resources to gain a recruit's trust

To gain a recruits trust, both the intelligence agency and the private intelligence officer must have these resources in abundance; money, power, drugs and sex. The intelligence officer must note the different personalities and their exploitable weaknesses and the resources that best suits in running them.

Money

The very act of recruiting spies need money and lots of it. It is impossible to buy sex, influence or drugs without money. The intelligence officer might have to buy some components of the op or elements that could motivate the recruit. Whether or not the recruit is a spy for ideological reasons or greed, money will play a big role at some point. For drug lords and those organizations into illicit business, a huge sum might be bribed for a certain piece of information and the recruit might be motivated by the sum. The recruit can also be paid with drugs, weapons, other assets in exchange for a desired action or result. For example, a certain individual needs to wipe his records clean and that will be the motivation.

Drugs

The case officer can use a wide variety of drugs in many different ways as a tool for recruitment and continued service. He could use alcohol (or cocktails of drugs) which is legal in most countries of the world. He'll try to get the recruit relaxed enough to spill the beans without giving himself out.

The intelligence officer or operative could use the following
strategies to stay sober:

- Before the meeting, which will include consumption of alcohol, he might eat a sizable quantity of fatty food. For instance, eat several pieces of bread heavily spread with butter or a pint of ice cream, so he doesn't get drunk himself (after all he needs a clear mind).
- He will make an arrangement with the bartender to control the drinks, mixing heavy drinks for the target and well-diluted drinks for him. For this, the bartender must be on his payroll or the meeting should be conducted in a place where he is in control.
- He would lift the glass to the lips, but would actually just sip the drink.
- He will proactively notice when the target's glass is empty, and orders another.
- He pretends to be more drunk than he actually is.

The aim of the above is to stay sober while the subject gets drunk, to loosen his lips. If the target has a drug addiction, the case officer might be able to use that knowledge to blackmail him or he might offer to supply the addict with the drug of his choice to loosen him, same as above; as a way of making friends or even as a means of rewarding the recruit for services rendered. It may even be possible for the case officer or one of his agents to introduce the potential recruit to drugs and then encourage an addiction which the case officer can later use to his advantage.

Unfortunately, this is the most common way girls are introduced to white slavery. The girls are abducted, made into heroin addicts, and forced to have sex in which they get paid with drugs and a little money. Although this illegal drugs might be great for building trust but it would also make the recruit careless in carrying out his information theft and he might sell out to someone else for the drugs too.

Security

The security officer must take every necessary step to make sure that the spy's position in the target organization is secured, such that the people who are the target of the intelligence operation do not learn that there is a spy within the ranks, and even if they do find out? There is no trace back to the case officer or organization. The case officer would need to observe these three important steps. He must set up procedures for handling the spy that accomplish the following objectives:

* Establish security procedures that the recruit will follow to avoid attracting attention to himself as he steals information.

* Establish secure methods of communication between the case officer and the spy or operative.

* Reduce personal contacts between the case officer and the spy to the absolute minimum required to maintain discipline, morale, and operational integrity.

As you can see, not all actionable intelligence should be used. Sometimes they are decoys or baits to flush out leaks and moles within the organization. The enemy target organization may leak out controlled information to different sets of people.

Whichever information leaks? Will directly lead to the rat in that organization. Another thing worth noting is the multi layered protection inherent in intelligence operations. In a lot of cases, its absolutely crucial for the recruit or spy to be deniable and must not trace back to the case officer or that organization. If in the event the case officer is traced? It ends there. The link should not go back to the parent organization. Depending on the complexity of the organizational structure, a lot of times these independent groups or cells are organized with 5 to 10 people in each cell depending on the specs of the mission or the Op. If you compromise one cell, other cells are operational and untouched.

SECURITY MEASURES

The case officer should provide recommended security procedures for the recruit as well as sufficient training to assist in information gathering and to avoid detection-- which is a consistent threat with the work he is involved in. InfoSec or information security also has to be in place to protect data from going to the wrong hands. Counterintelligence efforts or elements also exist because enemy groups may also have a campaign against you.

Eavesdropping is the safest method for stealing secrets in which the spy can participate in. The spy may attend meetings where intelligence worthy information is discussed, regularly overhear conversations near the desk where he works, or type up secret reports for the boss. In addition to what he hears and sees, the spy on the inside will have regular access to documents containing sensitive information. He might hold such documents in his private office during work hours and perhaps even in an office safe. He may even take documents home to work on. This sort of spying is low to medium risk spying, because the spy is doing his job or playing the role that the target expects him to assume. The risk there is when he tries to access information of which he is not authorized, and gets caught. For example, trying to use an office mate's computer to steal information. The solution to that is pretext. Before you do anything out of bounds or out of character, you must formulate a foolproof pretext or alibi or story that explains the action you are undertaking should you get caught. Always assume you will get caught so the explanation should be solid. Produce evidence beforehand. Another issue is how many have access to that information? Overtime they might deduce who the traitor is. Be aware of tests and deliberate leaks, which traceroute the spy or leaks in an organization.

Rick Ames was such a dangerous spy. He went to work every day and did exactly what he was supposed to do—and passed on everything to the KGB.
The better such a spy plays the role of the loyal, hardworking employee, or the grand but not demanding lover, the more he becomes the invisible person who makes a perfect spy. The risks of discovery increase when the spy must eavesdrop on conversations he is not supposed to hear, such as a secretary listening in on phone conversations or a chauffeur rewiring a connection so that he can listen to conversations in the backseat (even when the passengers have turned off the intercom). This risky but often necessary behavior includes deliberately gaining access to documents the spy would not normally see in the course of a workday. A

secretary might read documents on the boss' desk while he's in the bathroom, a file clerk might search through file cabinets that belong to an officer, or a chauffeur might open a briefcase left on the backseat while the employer goes to a meeting. These kinds of spies will need the most training and support from their control officers, not just on how to steal secrets, but also on how to keep their activities hidden, how to protect what they have stolen from discovery, and how to deliver said materials safely to the control officer (dead drops, brush pass etc.).In such situations the spy should never steal documents, but should instead copy them or photograph them. If that is impossible, the spy should read the documents and write a summary from memory as quickly as possible. Be aware and versed on ALL brands and models of commercial and military grade surveillance cameras, and how they may be customized. Also learn how to detect them. Everything nowadays is captured and recorded. That is one of the greater threats now for operatives, that did not exist decades ago. Fortunately, electronic countermeasures and detectors are also available. Such as these babies.(I am not connected with them in any way)

https://independentlivingnews.com/2013/11/12/20397-9-counter-surveillance-tools-you-can-legally-use/

The Art of Memorization

For a spy, memorization is an important technique that must be mastered at all times. He must also remember what he has heard or seen, sometimes for up to several hours, before he can find an opportunity to write the details down. Therefore, it is critical for the spy to develop the ability to memorize large quantities of information quickly, even during stress. In a pinch, to avoid being caught with incriminating written evidence the spy could use lemon juice or invisible ink in encoding his messages such that they will be seen only when exposed to heat or encoding it in a manner in which it will not be easy to decode. Well, they are easy and elementary to decode, but its better than nothing.

Documentation

The spy might be unable to photocopy the documents at the locations they are kept, so the spy might have to extract the document to a different location to copy it and then return it later. In his years as a spy, John Walker repeatedly made photocopies of code books and carried them home in his briefcase and never came close to getting caught. Also a smart spy might hide important documents in the midst of unsuspecting files such as a child's homework or a birthday invitation. Also, the spy might want to take recorders into meetings to record important information. Also a mobile phone camera is useful in so many ways , with all the apps available. But some organizations that handle classified information prohibit the use of electronics, camera or even mobile devices.

Computer storage

Most computer security programs are designed to keep strangers out of the system. But the whole purpose of recruiting a spy is to have someone gain access to a system. A knowledgeable computer expert can easily hack and gain access into many, but not all reserved areas. Better yet for the spy, those who have access to the sensitive areas of the network who are careless in keeping passwords a secret. They may write passwords down in a notebook; use easily discovered passwords such as their mothers' names, their addresses, or their birth dates; or get sloppy about checking to make sure that no one, not even their trusted secretaries, is looking over their shoulders when they log in. There is also the area of social engineering hacking which uses psychology, persuasion, trickery and pretexting to gain access to passwords.

If you're dealing with soft targets, then it is also easy to smuggle the stolen documents out of the office. Computer disks, memory cards can be hidden in a pocket, the inside of an electronic device, slipped into the lining of a coat, taped to the inner thigh, or put into an envelope and mailed out of the building. The information can also even be encrypted (highly recommended), then sent out as e-mail, or uploaded somewhere either as a document embedded as an image file. The computer in the spy's home or workplace can also be used as hiding places for stolen digital information, but it's highly discouraged because of the digital footprint it leaves, which can easily be investigated and found out by computer forensic experts. Any intelligence agent intending to use a computer as part of an intelligence-collection operation should go through the following checklist:

* Don't save or store any documents you want to keep secret on the hard disk or memory cards without high-level, military grade encryption. Always work on plain text documents in RAM memory and encrypt before storing the information on disks. There is software is available specially for this purpose of cleaning digital footprints, purging of any incriminating evidence. Also make sure there is a dependable way to

easily destroy data at a moment's notice. And such data must not be recoverable, even with the best computer forensic experts. That's why in Mission Impossible, you see self-destruct devices; it is for the purpose of safeguarding information. Also take note that password cracking even against military grade encryption will eventually succeed. It just is a question of processing power and time. So do bear that in mind with regards to passwords and that it will only buy you time, they are not enough to protect sensitive information permanently.

* Always use a total erase program when deleting any sensitive file from a hard disk on storage devices that you or your spy controls. Please note that most commercial versions, easily downloaded from some website or the App Store are not good enough. They have to be military grade if you really want to be protected.

* Keep all sensitive information in encrypted format on portable, easily concealed storage devices rather than the hard disk drive, and have a good, but accessible hiding place.

* Most encryption systems sold on the market can be easily broken, including many advertised as unbreakable systems. Many of the encryption systems bundled with word processor software are not secure. Know what makes an encryption program trustworthy.

* Even if you are sure you have the best encryption program available, double-encrypt everything, using two different systems.

* If you are sending messages online, always use an encryption system based on the RSA analog and a public key code. Among the best of these programs is Pretty Good

Privacy, which can be found on many computer bulletin boards for free.

* Change passwords frequently. The advantage of the RSA encryption system is that the public key passwords can be changed daily and given out in an open message. Never be too complacent and obvious in your passwords. In fact, I'd recommend password generators that spit out meaningless text.

* Be aware that it is possible to read a computer screen from a distance of up to several hundred feet with equipment that one can put together in a garage. Always take steps to ensure your computer is isolated and electromagnetic emissions are minimized.

Securing the Stolen Information

Every spy must have a safe house for storing information in case of emergencies. The spy must have a secure place both temporary (a false drawer) and permanent (a floor cabinet or a safety deposit box) to hide reports, photos, film, documents, computer disks, and anything else he might steal until they can be safely delivered to the case officer. The spy should have at least one temporary spot in every location. A flower vase, a spot in the backyard. These hiding places should be as secure as possible while still remaining inconspicuous. Although, it is recommended to make it is far away from your home or office as possible, but is nonetheless highly accessible to you. By accessible, it means you have a reason to be going there should someone tail you. Taping the memory disks under the sink in public toilets for example or public benches et cetera.

BRIDGING THE COMMUNICATION GAP BETWEEN THE CASE OFFICER AND THE SPY

The spy and case officer would need a secure and peculiar means of communicating and passing across information to each other. The means could vary from a visual signal to technological. Regardless of the situation of the spy activity (high or low threat security situation), the case officer should not be identified with the spy or agent he's running. Again, the necessity of pretext and alibis. Should they get caught, they should be able to easily explain it away with a solid legend or back story why both people are in that location and why they are talking to one another.

Less threatening situations

Recruitment and managing spies in relatively low-threat situations involving private parties or commercial businesses will generally not involve the extreme communications procedures described above. Nevertheless, there is always a chance that the target of the spy operation will identify the recruit as someone who may be spying against it. If that happens, the target organization's CI or Counterintelligence officers will attempt to follow the spy and identify who is the principal or receiving the stolen material. Therefore, even in a low-threat situation, the case officer must not allow anyone to identify him as someone who has regular contact with the spy if he has no good reason to be meeting with him.

Visible Contact

Method of communicating is simple as meeting in common areas like the park, with
the spy giving a signal such as crossing of the legs or on a jogging trail where the case
worker and the spy can easily pass and exchange information (brush pass). It could
even be in a church gathering where documents could be passed across with people
thinking it's just the church hymnal.

Point of Exchange

Information could be exchanged in many forms without any risk to the operatives. It
could be exchanged through the bathroom stall, in a mall where the spy drops the info
in the case officers cart, in a train station with both of them exchanging trains, or just
like in the movies, in which they both carry similar suitcases and they are exchanged.
In the movies though, the very fact you are carrying a conspicuous metallic silver
suitcase may not be the best idea. The principle is sound though. Just choose items
that are common to begin with i.e. grocery bags, newspapers, starbucks drink and etc.

Courier Service

Materials sent through this service are usually encoded and use ciphers. Intelligence
officers sometimes prefer to use couriers--usually support operatives, to carry
information back and forth between case officers and their recruits. Sometimes they
even make use of commercial courier services. An example where this setup can work
is through a cover of selling items online for example. This is practical and
inconspicuous too.

Mail Service

Due to the massive amount of junk mail that is dumped into every mailbox in the country, it is easy for a case officer to send messages to a spy which are designed to look like junk mail. Only the recruit will recognize the piece of mail as a message from his control officer. Such a scheme will usually involve secret writing and an encryption and decryption key. Passing an iron over the message or perhaps wiping the page with a chemical solution will bring out the secret message written in the margins are just some of the most basic examples. Microdots, were also heavily used decades ago in the cold war. The spy could also make use of the postal service of the government, embassy or at his workplace. He could drop a letter with a fake return address and some days later the case officer can pick it up. This can also be chained together. One message (using ciphers) will lead to a time specific instruction (say an ad in the newspaper), which will lead to another message, so on and so forth. It's a bit Nancy Drew, but you get the point I hope. You can make it as complex and have several steps (each requiring a different key or cipher) to decode each message.   You may also employ a decoy translation whereby the message will be decoded differently using a secondary key. A false message, in case the spy gets compromised along the chain.

Encoding the Telephone Communications

Telephone conversations are usually brief and highly encoded. They should sound like regular conversation of course. Extreme caution must be taken whenever talking on the telephone and one must assume that someone else is listening to every word. The following list of telephone security rules will keep the spy out of trouble.

- Do not discuss any illegal activity over any telephone to which you are known to
have access to. If you must make a call for such a purpose, make it from a public
phone to a public phone (this used to work well, but be aware CCTVs are everywhere
nowadays and public phones are becoming scarce, so this is near obsolete). This
means that arrangements must be made in advance so that the person receiving the
phone call will be monitoring the public phone when it rings.

- Whenever using a public phone or making sensitive calls from a private line, either
pay with coins or with a prepaid long-distance card, which can be purchased
anonymously in supermarkets, drugstores, and even the post office and cannot be
traced to you. (Remember that these pre-purchased telephone cards can be used to
make local calls, albeit at long-distance charges.)

- Remember that the easiest way to intercept and listen in on a telephone call is to
pick up an extension.

- Don't discuss sensitive information, even your credit card numbers, over any
cellular, cordless, or other type of phone that transmits a radio signal. Easily
intercepted using store bought scanners.

- Don't use obvious code words or trite phrases, such as calling cocaine "Coca Cola"
or talking about going on a "fishing trip" when the planned activity is a recruiting
session with a potential spy. If you find it necessary to talk in any kind of code, then
you should be sending encrypted messages through the most sophisticated encryption

systems available or commonly known as scramblers and again must sound like a normal conversation.

- If a phone must be used in an emergency, use a simple code to tell the other party to go to a prearranged public or safe phone and stand by to receive a call or to call a prearranged number. Have these default emergency protocols setup beforehand.

- Use burner phones. These are prepaid mobile phones you can buy anywhere. Unfortunately, you can use them only once, after that you need to throw them away. Not just the simcards, but the whole phone and everything! You can't resell them either, because some information can be retrieved by forensic technicians. Remember they are easy to trace, and make sure to disassemble or break them whenever possible, so that they cease transmitting any signal.

Cyphering your E- mail

The spy might encode information in a manner such that the caseworker alone can decode it. Messages can be sent through the Internet, commercial computer information services, private bulletin boards, or direct computer-to-computer connections. The problem with encrypted E- mail is the singular fact that it draws attention to itself as anyone who stumbles upon it would know it is hiding something. To avoid this some intelligence agencies now use self-destructive devices capable of destroying themselves after extraction of information or if an attempt to interpret it by the wrong person is detected. Mission Impossible! Its highly practical too.

KEEPING THE CONTACT MINIMAL

Personal contact between the case officer and the recruit should be kept at a minimum. The meeting might be for the spy to demand more money, explain challenges being faced, receive more training, relay information, or even to receive further instruction and mission orders. The case officer must remain in control at all times when it comes to arranging meetings, even at the times when it is the spy who is requesting for the personal contact. He must decide where and when to meet and how the recruit will travel to the meeting place. He should pick meeting places where he is totally familiar with the layout and the ordinary traffic through the area. This is to protect everyone. The case officer has the resources to sterilize the meet, but the spy will decide or at least suggest the when and where of the meet. At any point the spy can get caught and coerced to setup his handler in an ambush. Every time a meet is setup, everyone is subject to threats of being captured and the operation exposed.

Safe Houses

The safe house represents a place controlled by the case officer or any of his agents where the spy can go to in case of an emergency. It could be a ware house, an empty apartment close to the organization under surveillance. Usually the recruit is not aware of the safe house location until it is determined the spy needs to know by the case officer or handler.

Emotions and Stress Management

It is important for intelligence operatives to stay calm and confident during surveillance work. Fear, anger and other negative emotions may compromise an agent's ability to think on the fly, follow proper operating procedures, and maintain his cover. Stress may not only compromise an operative's mental capacity, but also his physical performance.

Mindful Meditation

Meditation is popularly known as a method for keeping the mind quiet, which is helpful for keeping the emotions and distracting thoughts down. Its basic procedure is to focus on an object (a point on the wall, a simple object or breathing) and keep the focus for 5 to 15 minutes. Beginners should take it easy and meditate for 3-5 minutes and gradually increase the duration as proficiency is gained.

Affirmations

Affirmations can be used to boost an operative's confidence as well as motivation to get the job done. Affirmations are positive statements, verbally conveyed to the self to bring up positive emotions. For agents to feel good before and during surveillance work, general affirmations can be used. These affirmations can be statements such as "I can do this", "This is easy", etc.

Emotional Freedom and Self Development Techniques

To get the best results, self-development techniques can be used to mentally and emotionally prepare the operative before going in the field. Among those proven to be effective in handling stress and negative emotions are Sedona method, EFT and self-hypnosis.

Pretexting

Pretexting is any activity which will entail assuming a story, roles and identities to facilitate an action, extract a particular action or result from targets or acquire specific information. When it comes to acquiring information, pretexting is almost necessary. It also serves as an escape route for surveillants when spotted, or questioned by counter intelligence parties. This is also used social engineering or getting confidential information, by hackers. In the movies, operatives posing as cable repairmen, or calling about an emergency are examples of pretexts.

Cover Identity

When the surveillant is spotted or questioned either by the subject or people around the area of operation, he should present a convincing cover story to get out of the situation. A cover story comes with a cover identity, which should be prepared before the operation. When deciding on a cover identity, it is ideal that the surveillance operatives use an identity type that is common in the area of surveillance, and will explain why he is there, and why he has all that equipment on hand.

Also, the investigator can use his cover identity to easily gain specific information. If the surveillance party were to acquire medical information of a person of interest, assuming the identity of a doctor would be the best option. If the investigator needs access to bank information, the identity of a bank clerk probably would be the best cover.

Furthermore, supporting accessories should be prepared such as identification cards, congruent clothes, real property, personal references such as pocket trash like torn bus tickets etc. to help sell the cover.

Cover Story or Legend

A cover story is all the information related to the background of your cover identity. Legends include the information about the cover identity's history, medical records, professional and educational background, etc. It is very important that every detail should be filled without leaving any informational gaps. The more resources you have to backstop or fabricate evidence or proofs supporting the cover or legend will cost more time, money and energy but could also mean the difference between life and death! These cover identities can be stolen, manufactured from scratch and to some extent hot-swappable. Pictures can easily be replaced and used by any other operative. This would depend on how the cover was built and sometimes may require a little appearance modification in order to look like the faked identity.

For example, a secondary operative, tasked to help create a street vendor legend? Will just need to keep his head down, make no strong connections with anyone, but enough people in the area would have to see him, including the CCTVs in the area. If Primary operative should need that legend for emergencies? He just needs to assume that identity until the cover is no longer necessary, so they can burn it.

A legend may be considered as an in-depth false alibi as to why the agent is at a particular place and at a particular time. Legends should be very convincing especially in odd situations such as getting caught at the front of a jewelry store at 2 a.m. or getting caught while trying to get into someone else's house. It is worth noting that every action should have a pre-text or a convincing reason that is congruent with the cover identity. How tight or waterproof the covers/legends are will depend on a case to case basis and resources and budgets available for the Op.

Backstop

A backstop refers to any arrangements or accessories that serve as proof to the agent's legend. Backstops are every important and may serve investigators well when an opposing party does a background check on the cover identities. An agent posing as a businessman would have a false business establishment with fake employees as his backstop. If the agent assigned to the task is posing as a foreigner is faking a degree in a university, his backstops would include citizen documents, phone number in the country of origin, fake relatives living in the native country, etc.

Foot Surveillance

When doing foot surveillance, it is best to use as many investigators as possible. This reduces the risk of getting caught by the subject. Foot surveillance typically uses up to 6 operatives (it can be more or less, again dependent on resources and if the subject is trained (hard target), with high situational awareness and counter surveillance measures. The street vendor example is an example of how one can disappear from surveillance. In most cases, one can successfully do foot surveillance with three investigators. Having 2 or more surveillance operators makes the operation less tiring as they can alternate staying within the proximity of the subject. An operative or two can drop out, if they feel the subject is getting close to detecting them.

One-man Surveillance

One-man foot surveillance should be avoided as much as possible. This is because it does not offer enough flexibility and may put the investigator at the risk of getting caught. If this type of surveillance needs to be done, the agent must stay behind the subject when moving on the same side of the street. To get a better look at what the subject is doing, stay close as possible without triggering any suspicion. It's crucial to master the layout of the places, the entry and exit points etc. of the environment. You can't be caught by surprise, because you don't have a team mate to re-acquire the subject, should you lose him. Take note that the operative should not invade the subject's personal space. When it comes to determining the right distance to maintain, it is usually dictated by the environmental condition the agent and the subject is in as well as the size and type of crowd within the area. The more crowded it is, the closer you need to be. If you're surveilling a subject in empty, well it places? You have to be totally invisible! Other factors that should be considered when determining the right distance from the target include light conditions, subject's actions, his awareness, his speed, complexity of the terrain, staggering number of entry and exit points, his skillsets, as well as the agent's goals.

In case the subject turns a corner into a street that is less crowded, do not make the mistake of following the subject. Instead, continue walking across the intersecting street. To make up for your compromising position, glance up to the street the subject is travelling and take note of his position, direction currently travelling, and actions. Operate from across the street.

If the subject turns a corner to a crowded street, simply stop at the corner. The agent can conduct observations, which should be done discreetly. If the subject is moving, the investigator can keep following the subject through the same side of the street. It should also be noted that no matter what the conditions are, the investigator should not turn immediately to a corner when following the subject to avoid detection. Moving over watch positions are also great, in case the ground operatives lose the target. These are operatives who take the high ground or over watch vantage points. Not always practical, but when available has a lot of advantages. Drones are also now becoming commonplace and can now be deployed for over watch.

When tailing a subject from across the street, the manner, which the agent follows the subject is entirely dependent on the circumstance. The operation can be done at the front of the subject, behind, or side-by-side (facing the same direction). In most cases, operating while walking side-by-side with the subject since it allows observation to be continued, even if the subject makes a sudden turn to a corner.

Two-man Surveillance

The two-man surveillance is also referred to as AB surveillance. The letters A and B are used to represent the two surveillants. In this surveillance technique, the agent designated as "A" is positioned behind the subject while the agent designated as "B" is directly behind A. In other words, A follows the subject while B follows A. When working on the same side of the street as the subject, in the subject turns a corner, A will go straight ahead without turning and cross the intersecting street as he communicates the direction of the subject to B. Agent B should not turn to the corner the subject has just turned to until he receives the signal from A.

If B is making observations across the street and the subject makes a turn (on the same side of the street), B will then cross the street, taking the original position of A while A takes the original position of B (across the street). This is a prearranged move, which does not require any signals. If the subject makes a turn to the opposite side of the street, B should slow down and avoid meeting the subject. B should keep A in sight and observe signals from A regarding the next move to take. By then, B can either go inside a store or stay at a non-suspicious spot.

Three-man Surveillance

The ABC or Three-man surveillance is designed to cover both sides of the subject. This is done with A following the subject; B follows A while staying anticipating signals A might send. In most cases, C does his observations across the street while keeping his position slightly at the rear of the subject. C should not turn his head while observing subject to avoid detection. Variants include having B and C across the street and having all three agents on the same side of the street.

In the ABC foot surveillance technique, having three agents is necessary to easily maneuver around the subject in areas that are crowded people or vehicles. If the subject makes a turn to a corner on the same side of the street, A will continue with the initial direction of movement, cross the intersecting street and sends signals to B and C on the next steps to take. The two agents (C or B) may also take up the original A position while A may take up the C position to continue his observation at the other side of the street. If the subject turns to a corner on the other side of the street, C will take the initial A position but should not take it without the go signal from A. Either A or B can take the original B position while the remaining agent will take the original C position.

Automobile Surveillance

It is necessary to do an automobile surveillance when the subject aboard a moving vehicle. This type of surveillance requires modified foot surveillance techniques. To gain success in this type of surveillance, a reliable vehicle should be used. The investigator should ensure that the license plate of the vehicle used for the surveillance is not identifiable. Two-way radios and other long-range communication devices can be helpful when using two or more vehicles for the operation. Certain considerations should be taken as well, including extra fuel, first aid kit, food/drinks, GPS navigation systems and road maps. It is highly recommended that at least two agents should be assigned in one surveillance vehicle.

Combining this surveillance with foot surveillance can be advantageous. In some cases, necessary. Doing automobile surveillance in conjunction with foot surveillance can help get rid of boredom and apathy in agents. Whenever the subject stops the vehicle and dismounts, one agent should dismount as well and resort to foot surveillance. If the subject stops and stays in the vehicle, another agent does foot surveillance, for better results. Having both surveillants in the vehicle while the subject's vehicle is parked should be avoided since a subject's accomplice may throw something on the subject's vehicle without being seen by the surveillants.

When doing vehicle surveillance, techniques should be changed every now and then to avoid getting caught. Changing one technique into another should be done discreetly. At times, it can be necessary to change the appearance of the investigators' vehicle. Making changes during the operation breaks the pattern of the trail – formation of a trailing pattern may expose the operation. Here are factors one may work on when making changes during operation:

- Driving speed
- Lanes the surveillants are travelling on. (Avoid traffic violations)
- Directions (around the block, opposite direction at the opposite lane, etc.)
- Passenger positions (crouching or changing positions can make it appear that the number of passengers in the vehicle has changed).
- Clothes
- Removable stickers, visual accessories (they can help alter the appearance of the vehicle).

During the night, it can be difficult to ensure that the investigators are tailing the right vehicle. This can be made easier if the subject's vehicle is distinctive. In case the subject's vehicle has a common design, a chance can be taken to attach a marker such as a reflector, or a sticker with a light color. Please note the availability of vehicle trackers, available in Amazon and Ebay. The risk is, if you install it? You also must covertly bring it back with you.

Decreasing the visibility of the surveillant's vehicle can contribute to the success of the operation as it decreases the chance of getting caught. However, this should be done without breaking the law. The interior lights in the surveillant's vehicle should be disconnected so it won't turn off when the door is open. The headlights and the license plate light can be set up so they can be turned on and off separately.

There are certain actions that surveillants should avoid. These actions include:

- Parking in the same spot for too long

- Vehicle occupants remaining in the same seat for a long time

- Sitting behind the steering wheel when the vehicle is parked

- Approaching and leaving parking vehicles in a sneaky manner (this can make a surveillant look suspicious)

- Using conspicuous vehicles (military vehicles, sports cars that stand out too much, vehicle designs that are out of place, etc.)

-Using shortwave radios without precautionary measures.

- Parking in reserved slots or "no parking" areas

- Using government cards in car service stations in surveillance operation areas

- Holding general conferences with other agents in the surveillance area

- Trying to hide or turning the vehicle in for the purpose of hiding one's face from the subject.

- Using the same phone to make multiple calls.

One-vehicle surveillance

When doing one-vehicle surveillance, the investigators' vehicle should remain as close to the subject's vehicle as possible to allow observation of the subject's actions. However, the surveillant should remain far enough to avoid getting detected. This is indeed a tricky endeavor.

When the subject's vehicle turns a corner, the surveillant may continue following the subject. Also, the investigator has two options: continue with the original direction, make a U-turn before turning to the corner the subject just went into (the target won't be interested in a vehicle taking a street behind him), or continue with the original direction and continue around the block (the target won't expect to be tailed a by vehicle coming from an opposite direction).

AB Surveillance

The two-vehicle surveillance is done the same way as AB type foot surveillance. A follows the subject while B follows A. If the subject makes a turn, A will continue with the original direction and let B, after receiving a go signal from A, follow the subject. The surveillants can communicate with each other through radio-transmitters. This technique can be modified; one surveillant vehicle can go to the same direction as the subject's on a parallel street. When tailing during long rides, the surveillant vehicles can switch places from time to time to avoid suspicion.

ABC Surveillance

This is done the same way that the foot surveillance technique of the same name is done. Except, the car designated as C uses a parallel route. If the subject makes a turn towards the location of C, the C will take the original position of A, while A or B takes the original position of A. If the subject makes a turn away from the position of C, A will proceed to the original direction and take a route parallel to the route of the subject while A or C takes the original position of A.

Leapfrog Technique

There are times when the party conducting an intelligence operation needs to be extra cautious. Hence, will need to take time and ensure that the surveillants are in a safe yet convenient position. The leapfrog technique can be very useful in such situations. To do this, have the investigators watch the subject from a fixed position until the target makes a move and do this technique. This is ideally done by more than 2 surveillance vehicles, since it involves waiting at predetermined locations (along the suspected route the subject is going to take. This method is generally safer and more discreet than techniques that involve tailing the subject. One of the obvious disadvantages to this technique is that it may take a long time and may require surveillants to stay in their assigned areas longer, until significant information is gathered.

Fixed Surveillance

In this type of surveillance, the target remains stationary in an observation post. This gives the investigator the option to get closer and do better observation at the target and at the area of surveillance. Having all the necessary equipment should not be taken for granted; it can increase the chance of operational success. They may include binoculars, sound recorders, cameras, and electronic aids. The operatives will need reliefs every now and then to keep up with the operation. Hence, specific arrangements should be made. Also, communication lines that go to the headquarters should be arranged and secured.

There will be cases when the investigator won't be able to observe the subject at a fixed location. He may need to assume a role that will help him get close to the subject without attracting unnecessary attention. Roles that the surveillant can assume include salesman, mailman, garbage collector, telephone technician, etc. Having disguised vehicles that can be used as observation posts in the area of surveillance should be considered.

As with all surveillance operations, investigators should avoid actions that may compromise the success of the operation. Surveillants should be dressed to blend in the environment. The use of equipment as well as the arrival and departure of the investigators should be done as discreetly as possible.

ONE LAST THING...

If you enjoyed this book or found it useful I'd be very grateful if you'd post a short review here. Your support really does make a difference and I read all the reviews personally so I can get your feedback and make this book even better.

If you'd like to leave a review, then all you need to do is click the review link on this book's page.

Thanks again for your support!

This guide is not intended as and may not be construed as an alternative to or a

substitute for professional business, mental counseling, therapy or medical services

and advice

The authors, publishers, and distributors of this guide have made every effort to

ensure the validity, accuracy, and timely nature of the information presented here

However, no guarantee is made, neither direct nor implied, that the information in this

guide or the techniques described herein are suitable for or applicable to any given

individual person or group of persons, nor that any specific result will be achieved

The authors, publishers, and distributors of this guide will be held harmless and

without fault in all situations and causes arising from the use of this information by

any person, with or without professional medical supervision The information

contained in this book is for informational and entertainment purposes only It not

intended as a professional advice or a recommendation to act

No part of this book may be reproduced or transmitted in any form whatsoever,

electronic, or mechanical, including photocopying, recording, or by any informational

storage or retrieval system without express permission from the author

Other books by JNR Publishing Group

The Art of Erasing Emotions: Techniques to discharge any emotional problems in men, women and children using EFT and Sedona

From Zero to a Fully Motivated Brain: a manifesto on self - motivation

The Seduction Force Multiplier 1 Bring Out Your FULL Seduction powers through the Power of Routines, Drills, Scripting and Protocols

Shielded Heart How To Stop Yourself From Falling For A Seduction Target

Secrets to Hacking Your Brain Be Your Own Therapist

The Art Of Virtual Practice 2 Learning and Mastery Of Any Skill At Lighting Speeds!

The Persuaders Guide To Eliminating Resistance And Getting Compliance

The Art of Invisible Compliance How To Make People Do What You Want Effortlessly

The TEN Game Operations Manual: How To Get Extremely Gorgeous 10s Consistently and Predictably!

How Not To Give a Shit!: The Art of Not Caring

Manipulative Eye Contact Techniques: Install thoughts and feelings just with your eyes!

The Injector Protocol: How To Inject Your Essence Literally Into Everything!

Tough Love: Surviving and Winning The Most Difficult Romance Games, Relationships and Lovers From Hell!

Seducing the UNseduceable Man: Specialized seduction techniques for the impossible to get man!

Be A Human Lie Detector: Detect HighLevel, Covert Communications of Persuaders, Seducers and Other Manipulators!

The Corporate Warriors Manual

Applying Military Principles to Conquer Business and Life!

The EQ Genius

Mastering Emotional Intelligence

The Art of Risk Management

Learn to Manage Risks Like a Pro

Make Your Own Affirmations, Autosuggestions and Self Hypnosis Products

Drastically Improve ANY Aspect of Your Life On Autopilot!

Printed in Great Britain
by Amazon

72700808R00031